Great Women of the BIBLE

Great Women of the Bible

The Princess and the Baby
Ruth and Naomi
The Queen Who Saved Her People

An ARCH BOOKS® Gift Collection

*An Inspirational Press Book
for Children*

First Inspirational Press edition published in 2000.

Inspirational Press
A division of BBS Publishing Corporation
386 Park Avenue South
New York, NY 10016

Inspirational Press is a registered trademark of BBS Publishing Corporation.

Published by arrangement with Arch® Books, a division of Concordia
Publishing House, 3558 S. Jefferson Avenue, St. Louis, Missouri 63118-3968.

Library of Congress Catalog Card Number: 99-96389

ISBN: 0-88486-267-4

Printed in Mexico.

The Princess and the Baby

EXODUS 1:8 – 2:10 FOR CHILDREN

Written by Janice Kramer

Illustrated by Sally Mathews

The wicked king of Egypt was
as worried as could be.
"Israelites!" he fumed and fussed.
"That's all I ever see!
They work our land.
They breathe our air.
Those Israelites are everywhere!
If I'm not careful, some fine day
they'll up and take my land away!

"I'll make them suffer. Then they'll leave,
and Egypt will be mine.
Those Israelites will know this king
is not without a spine!"
He made them carry stones and sticks
and great big heavy loads of bricks.
And worst of all, he planned to kill
the baby boys of Israel!

Oh, what a wicked man he was
to think of such a thing!
But many of the Israelites
were smarter than the king.
They hid their baby boys from sight
and kept them hidden day and night.
They prayed and prayed that God above
would help them with His strength and love.

One mother tried to keep her baby
quiet as a mouse.
But every day the soldiers
of the king rode by her house.
"If he should cry as they pass by,
they'll know he's here, and he will die.
My baby must be kept alive!
Somehow, someway he must survive!"

And so that loving mother made
a tiny little boat.
With loving care she made it strong
so it was sure to float.
She dressed her baby in his clothes,
then kissed him on his little nose
and tucked him in with blankets round
to keep him warm and safe and sound.

The baby's sister Miriam
was puzzled through and through.
"Why, Mother!" cried the little girl,
"What *are* you going to do?"
"You'll see," the mother said, "You'll see.
Be quiet now and follow me."
Then out the door with cautious eye
she looked for soldiers passing by.

The way was clear. She gathered up
her baby, boat and all.
"Stay right beside me, Miriam.
Be careful not to fall."
They walked together one long mile
until they reached the River Nile.
And then the little girl began
to understand her mother's plan.

And when they reached the river's edge,
they put the strong boat in,
then laid the baby down inside.
No water touched his skin.
He didn't cry or make a peep,
he simply yawned and went to sleep.
The mother wiped away a tear.
"The king will never find him here."

"Oh, Mother," said the little girl,
"I'll stay with him all day.
If anyone should come, I'll just
pretend I'm here to play."
The mother kissed her daughter's face
and held her in a long embrace.
"My little girl," she said with pride,
"has suddenly grown up inside!"

With that the mother hurried home;
she had been gone too long.
Now would the soldiers start to think
that something had gone wrong?
Poor Miriam was all alone.
She sat for hours on a stone
and watched the baby slumber on.
How strange it seemed with Mother gone!

Then suddenly she heard a sound
upon the river path.
"Three ladies!" whispered Miriam.
"They've come to take a bath!
Oh, no! The one that's chattering,
she is the daughter of the king.
He murders little baby boys.
I mustn't make a single noise!"

She ducked and hid, but all was lost—
they'd seen the little boat!
"Why, look!" the princess cried aloud.
"A little baby boy afloat!"
She picked him up, and how he cried!
"An Israelite," the princess sighed.
"But he's so sweet, as sweet can be.
I'll take him home to live with me!"

The ladies hadn't noticed
that young Miriam was there.
So she approached them now as if
she didn't have a care.
"Hello!" she said. "I'm almost nine.
And don't you think the weather's fine?
What have you there? Why, goodness me!
Is that a baby boy I see?"

"Why, yes, it is," the princess said.
"I found him floating over there."
"You'll need a nurse," said Miriam,
"to give him proper care.
I know a lady Israelite
who'd nurse him for you day and night."
The princess answered thankfully,
"Please go and bring her here to me."

When Miriam came back, she had
her mother by the hand!
Then bowing low, the mother said,
"I'll do what you command."
The princess looked at her and smiled.
"I'll pay you well to nurse this child.
Take care of him until he's grown,
and love him as your very own."

The mother's eyes were filled with tears.
Her heart was filled with joy.
She praised the Lord for giving back
her little baby boy.
And Miriam was happy too,
for deep within her heart she knew
there must have been some reason why
God hadn't let her brother die.

DEAR PARENTS:

Our story ends with the thought that Miriam was happy, "for deep within her heart she knew there must have been some reason why God hadn't let her brother die." We know from later chapters in Exodus that Miriam lived to see the reason why God saved Moses.

As a young prince in the Pharaoh's court Moses learned the ways of a leader. He received a good education. Yet Moses did not forget the suffering of his people under the hand of Pharaoh. One day he came to the defense of an Israelite and killed an Egyptian. He had to run for his life.

Forty years later God appeared to Moses in a burning bush and called him to be the leader of His people. He obeyed the Lord. He spoke His Word and led the people of Israel from slavery in Egypt through the waters of the Red Sea to freedom and to the borders of the Promised Land.

We, too, can see the wonder of God's plan in the life of Moses. We can also see the fulfillment of His plan in Jesus Christ. Like Moses, the young Child Jesus was saved from death. God led Joseph and Mary to take Him to Egypt to escape the sword of Herod's soldiers. Later Jesus suffered and died for us and rose again to crush the power of sin and death.

Help your child to sense the wonder of God's love in His great plan and to live in the security that He cares for each of His children today.

THE EDITOR

Ruth AND Naomi

The Book of Ruth FOR CHILDREN

Written by Anne Jennings
Illustrated by Vaccaro Associates

Former Title: A STORY FOR OBED

"Young Obed, you are eight today,"
Said Grandma Naomi.
"Have you a wish that I could grant?
I'll do so happily."
"Tell me a story!" Obed cried.
"Of course!" old Naomi replied.

'I'll tell you one I love to repeat
Of how your parents happened to meet.
You'll like it. Here, sit down, young man.
And hear just how it all began.

"It was like this: For many months
No gentle rain at all
In great and lovely silver drops
On Bethlehem would fall.

In Israel we could not stay.
Our family had to move away
And live, for many days and nights,
Among the friendly Moabites."
"How long?" the boy asked eagerly.
"For ten whole years," said Naomi.

"What happened then?" he wished to know.
"My husband and my sons were dead.
I started back for Bethlehem
And my old home," she said.
"Now one dead son had left a wife,
A Moabite who joined her life
With ours, although a foreigner.
Her name was Ruth, and we loved her.

My journey had not yet begun
When Ruth said, 'Mother, we are one.
And you and I must never part.
You know that you have all my heart.
The same bright sun on us will shine;
Your God, your people shall be mine!'

"When we arrived in Bethlehem,
We had no food to eat.
Ruth gathered up the fallen grains
Of barley and of wheat
In rich Boaz's ripened field.

Ruth made some flour with the yield.
Boaz watched eagerly and then
Invited her to come again.
And that, young Obed, don't forget,
Is how your own two parents met!"

"I like that story!" Obed cried.
"I'm very glad to know
That Ruth, my mother, came with you
Because she loved you so."
"It was God's will," said Naomi,
"That she should follow, willingly.
It was God's will, I now repeat,
That she and good Boaz should meet.
But let me tell you what he said
Before he and your mother wed.

"One day I watched the workmen as
They gathered up the sheaves
And stored them in Boaz's barn
Right to the very eaves.
I saw Ruth gather, busily,
With movements neat as they could be,
The grains the workers left behind,
As Boaz wished, for her to find.
Her gentle voice, then his, I heard.
I understood each single word.

"She spoke. 'I am a stranger here.
Why are you kind to me?'
'I'm kind because you've won my heart
By your good deeds,' said he.

And then he left her all alone.
She stood there as if turned to stone
And looked before her, did not speak,
A lovely blush upon each cheek,
Bright as a red-gold ray of sun
At evening, when the day is done.

"When all the grain was gathered and
The harvest sun hung high
Like a great golden blessing in
The lovely autumn sky,
Ruth and the good Boaz were wed.

I cried for joy, then bowed my head
And thanked God for the splendid son
And daughter dear whom I have won.
Boaz and Ruth and I, we three,
Then lived together, happily.

"God blessed our work and made each day
A time of simple joy.
Then you were born, to make us glad,
A handsome baby boy.

And we believe—we're sure it's true
That God has special plans for you."
"What plans?" he cried. "Boaz's son
Will be the forerunner of One
Who will come down from heaven above
To teach the world to live in love."

The boy had listened, thoughtfully,
To old Naomi's word.
Her story was the very best
That he had ever heard.
He liked the bright thought of the birth
Of Him who should bring love to earth;
And then he spoke with great delight
The name of Ruth, the Moabite,
Who'd lived, and so unselfishly,
A life of love for Naomi.

DEAR PARENTS:

So often today poor Naomi gets left out of the story of Ruth. Popular wedding songs and the like lead us to believe that "whither Boaz went, Ruth would go." But it was to Naomi that Ruth gave her love, and *Ruth and Naomi* will give your child a chance to get this straight.

The fact that Naomi was only Ruth's mother-in-law and of a different nationality besides makes the girl's love all the more remarkable. And her love was certainly rewarded, for among the "alien corn" she found another husband to cherish her and a position in the royal lineage of the King of Kings. How God must have loved *her!*

He loves us with the same unfailing love and sent His Son Jesus to ask us to be followers too—followers of Him. He promises that all along our journey and at its end we will find treasures richer even than Ruth's.

Talk to your child about how we act toward someone we really love. Why do we want to be with them? Why do we want to do kind things for them? Why do we want them to be happy? Explain that this is how Ruth felt about Naomi, and it is also how God feels about us. He *is* with us all the time. He gave us the kindest Gift of all, His Son, so that we can be happy forever. His is the greatest love of all!

THE EDITOR

THE QUEEN WHO SAVED HER PEOPLE

Book of Esther FOR CHILDREN

Illustrated by Jack Glover

Written by Carol Greene

In long-ago Persia, a land like a dream,
King Ahasuerus decreed that the cream
of all the young maidens be brought to his throne,
and from them he promised to choose one alone.
She'd reign as his queen, and she'd be his dear wife.
(What girl wouldn't love to live that sort of life?)

A kind Jewish servant called Mordecai peered
at the young girls arriving and stroked his long
  beard.
"From far and from near they have come by the
  dozen,
but none are so lovely as Esther, my cousin.

"I'll take her to Ahasuerus' hall,
and if it's God's will, he'll choose her over all."

The folk in the palace all loved Esther dearly,
and soon came the day when the king announced
    clearly,
"It's Esther I've chosen above all the rest."
"Hurrah!" cried the crowd. "He has chosen the
    best!"

The whole kingdom stopped work to honor their
    queen
with feasts such as never before had been seen.

At first life was sweet for the happy young bride.
Then Haman, a prince who was puffed up with
    pride,
in some sneaky way got the king to decree:
"Now Haman's head servant; to him bend your
    knee!"

The other poor servants just had to obey,
and Mordecai stroked his long beard with dismay,

"Jews bow to their God," said the gentle old man.
"Bow down before Haman? There's no way I can!"

When Haman found this out, he narrowed his eyes
and ran to the king with a whole pack of lies.
The king, all befuddled, at last said, "Okay!
You're head servant, Haman. We'll do it your way."
And what was the terrible thing Haman planned?
To kill every Jew in the whole Persian land!

Now tears of despair flowed from Mordecai's eyes.
Each street that he wandered was filled with his
cries.
It seemed from such evil could never come good.
Then God's Spirit touched him, and he understood:

Queen Esther was Jewish! God gave her that throne so her people would not face their trouble alone.

A servant told Esther about Haman's plan.
"Oh, no!" cried the queen. "What a horrible man!
I'll stop him, I promise! I know what I'll do:
Have a feast for the king and invite Haman too.
And when the king's happy, his tummy quite full,
I'll tell him the trick Haman thought he could pull."

The feast was soon ready, the candles burned
 bright,
but Esther somehow felt the time was not right.
"I'll have them tomorrow to another great feast
And *then* tell the king that his servant's a beast."

So next day the cooks did the whole thing again.
The queen and her guests ate and ate and ate. Then,

"I've something to ask you, dear Ahasuerus,"
said Esther. "Is there any chance that you'll spare
    us?
Would you have your queen killed and her people
    too?

I thought that you loved me. Please tell me you do!"
At first the king thought she was just having fun.
But then Esther told him what Haman had done.

"He *what*?!" cried the king, and did Haman shake then,
and soon no one saw him, not ever again.

Good Mordecai took over Haman's old job.
He wisely and happily ruled the whole mob
of servants, who now liked to cook and to clean.
"Our life's so much better. It's thanks to the queen!"

Then all of the Jews in the whole Persian land held a thanksgiving feast; 'twas the first ever planned.

"We thank God for Esther. To Him we sing praise!

"We'll thank Him and trust Him the rest of our
    days."
And Jews to this day every year read the tale
of Esther, who showed them God's love will not
    fail.